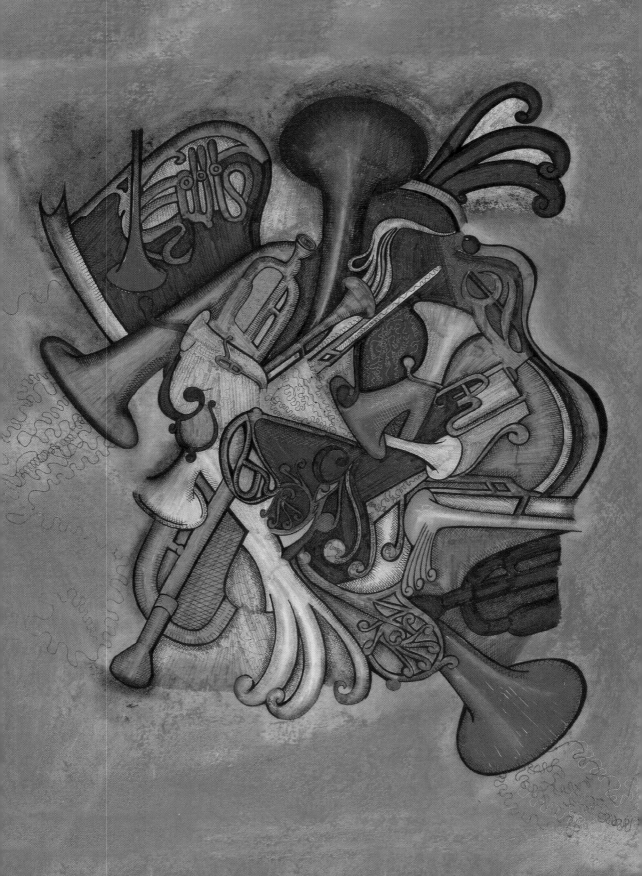

Am I Musical?
Discover Your Music Potential
(Adults and Children Ages 7 and Up)

Music Audiation Games

Edwin E. Gordon

GIA Publications, Inc.
Chicago

Am I Musical?

Discover Your Music Potential
(Adults and Children Ages 7 and Up)
Music Audiation Games

Jacket design and illustration by Yolanda Durán
Book design and illustration by Yolanda Durán

G-6092
ISBN: 1-57999-222-6
Copyright © 2003 GIA Publications, Inc.
7404 S. Mason Ave., Chicago, IL 60638
www.giamusic.com

Table of Contents

Music Audiation Games

About the Artwork

Artist Yolanda Durán, in her inspired illustrations throughout this book, shows with whimsy and grace that music is nourishment to the soul.

If music be the food

of love, play on.

Twelfth Night, Act i, Sc. 1
William Shakespeare

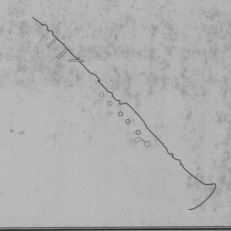

Only the pure in heart
can make a good soup.

— *Ludwig Van Beethoven*

It's easy to play any musical instrument: all you have to do is touch the right key at the right time and the instrument will play itself.

—J.S.Bach

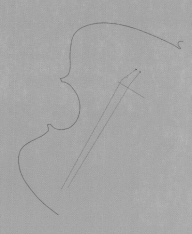

If you can walk you can dance. If you can talk you can sing.

—*Zimbabwe Proverb*

Music is a primary condition
of the human experience. In
the history of man on earth,
many civilizations have been
identified that could not
read, write, or calculate.
None have been discovered
that did not make music.

—*Eugene Corporon*

Am I Musical?
Music Audiation Games

Purpose of the Games

You have probably wondered at one time or another whether you or your children have music potential, or the inborn capacity to learn music. The fact is that everyone has at least some potential to learn and enjoy music. Audiation, which is to music what thought is to language, is the basis of music potential. To understand the extent of that potential is to be well informed, particularly about the appropriate way to learn music in accord with your and/or your child's individual musical needs and differences.

If a person has attained a high degree of performance in singing or playing a musical instrument, such achievement has its basis in high music potential. But musical potential alone, regardless of degree and unlike musical achievement, is not so easily observed. Unfortunately, because so many people have never had music lessons, they are neither able nor encouraged to demonstrate their musical potential.

This is where the "Am I Musical?" Games come into play. The purpose of the games is to objectively reveal a general estimate of the extent of musical potential that you and/or your child possess. No formal education in music is required to play the games.

The result of the games must not be considered absolute. Many factors contribute to one's music potential, and it is not intended that all factors will be accounted for in the games. In a relative sense, high scores may be taken seriously, whereas average and low scores require additional investigation. Above all, regardless of results, no one should be deprived of participating in music activities of his or her choice. You may compile more specific information by using a supplementary standardized test of music aptitudes. The names of tests, their purposes, and the chronological ages they are designed for are explained later in this booklet.

Description of the Games

Am I Musical? has two parts: 1) the Adult Game, and 2) the Youth Game. The Adult Game is designed for persons ages 13 and over, and the Youth Game is designed for children ages 12 and under. If one game is too easy or too difficult, then the other game should be played. It takes approximately 12 minutes to complete each game.

There are 40 questions in each game. The questions in both the Adult Game and the Youth Game are the same, but directions for the games are different. Colored answered sheets, recorded directions on a CD, musical explanations, and practice exercises accompany each game.

The Youth Game

The object of the Youth Game is to listen to and remember a four-second long *Model Song*. After the song is played, it is compared one at a time to other short songs of the same length. When the other song being played sounds like the *Model Song*, go to the number of that song on the answer sheet and fill in the circle located underneath the S (which stands for same). When the other song being played does not sound like the *Model Song*, fill in the circle located underneath the NS (which stands for not the same). The other song may not sound the same because the melody, rhythm, or harmony is changed. There is never more than one type of change in each song.

The *Model Song* is played at the beginning of the game and in between every two questions in order to help you remember it. The word *Model* is announced each time the *Model Song* is played.

The Adult Game

The Adult Game is designed and played just like the Youth Game with one exception: During the Adult Game, if a song does not sound like the *Model Song*, then you are asked to specify exactly what makes the song different. For example, if the melody is different, then the circle under melody is filled in, if the rhythm is different, then the circle under rhythm is filled in, and if the harmony is different, then the circle under harmony is filled in. Musical examples of what the words *melody, rhythm,* and *harmony* mean are included in the recorded directions.

Although the directions for each game are recorded on the CD, you may find it helpful for yourself or your child to actually read the directions before you hear them. They are written on the next page.

Recorded Directions for the Youth Game

- Listen to this *Model Song*. You will hear it performed many times. You will also hear other songs. The game is to decide if the song you hear performed is the same or not the same as the Model Song. If it is not the same as the *Model Song*, it will sound different in one of three ways.

- Listen to the *Model Song* again. Listen to the first way it may sound different. Listen to the second way it may sound different. Listen to the third way it may sound different.

- If you hear the *Model Song* performed, you will fill the circle under Same on your answer sheet. If the song you hear is not the same as the *Model Song,* you will fill the circle under Not Same on your answer sheet.

- By this time, the *Model Song* should sound familiar. But to be sure, listen to it once again. Look at your answer sheet and find the word Practice and number 1.

  - Listen to Practice 1 and mark your answer. If you filled the circle under Same, that is correct, because what you heard is the same as the *Model Song.*

  - Listen to Practice 2, find Practice 2 on your answer sheet, and mark your answer. If you filled the circle under Not Same, that is correct, because what you heard is not the same as the *Model Song.*

  - Listen to the *Model Song* again to help you remember what it sounds like, but do not mark your answer sheet after the word Model. Just listen.

  - Listen to Practice 3, find Practice 3 on your answer sheet, and mark your answer. If you filled the circle under Not Same, that is correct, because what you heard is not the same as the *Model Song*.

- Listen to Practice 4, find Practice 4 on your answer sheet, and mark your answer. If you filled the circle under Not Same, that is correct, because what you heard is not the same as the *Model Song*.

■ You are now ready to play the game. The number for each song will be announced before the song is performed. When you see the word Model on your answer sheet, that means the *Model Song* will be played to help you remember what is sounds like. Do not make a mark after the word Model. Just listen.

■ To begin, find the word *Begin* and number 1 on your answer sheet. Listen carefully to song number 1. Then fill the circle under Same or Not Same after number 1. Mark your answers quickly so that you will be ready to listen to the next song.

Recorded Directions for the Adult Game

■ Listen to this *Model Song*. You will hear it performed many times. You will also hear other songs. The game is to decide if the song you hear is the same as the *Model Song* or different from the *Model Song*. If it is different from the *Model Song,* it could be for one of three reasons. The melody may be different, the rhythm may be different, or the harmony may be different.

■ Listen to the *Model Song* again. Its melody alone sounds like this….Its rhythm alone sounds like this….Its harmony alone sounds like this….Now listen to the *Model Song* again with all three parts—the melody, rhythm, and harmony—performed together.

- If you hear the *Model Song* performed, you will fill the circle under Same on your answer sheet. If you hear a different melody, you will fill the circle under *Melody* on your answer sheet. If you hear a different rhythm, you will fill the circle under *Rhythm* on your answer sheet. If you hear a different harmony, you will fill the circle under *Harmony* on your answer sheet. When a song sounds different, it will be for only one reason: melody, rhythm, or harmony.

- By this time, the *Model Song* should sound familiar. But to be sure, listen to it once again. Look on your answer sheet and find the word Practice and number 1.

  - Listen to Practice 1 and mark your answer. If you filled the circle under Same, that is correct, because what you heard is the same as the *Model Song*.

  - Listen to Practice 2, find Practice 2 on your answer sheet, and mark your answer. If you filled the circle under Melody, that is correct, because the melody is different from the *Model Song*.

  - Listen to the *Model Song* again to help you remember what it sounds like, but do not mark your answer sheet after the word Model. Just listen.

  - Listen to Practice 3, find Practice 3 on your answer sheet, and mark your answer. If you filled the circle under Rhythm, that is correct, because the rhythm is different from the *Model Song*.

  - Listen to Practice 4, find Practice 4 on your answer sheet, and mark your answer. If you filled the circle under Harmony, that is correct, because the harmony is different from the *Model Song*.

- You are now ready to play the game. The number for each song will be announced before the song is performed. When you see the word Model on your answer sheet, that means the *Model Song* will be played to help you remember what it sounds like. Do not make a mark after the word Model. Just listen.

- To begin, find the word *Begin* and number 1 on your answer sheet. Listen carefully to song number 1. Then fill the circle under *Same, Melody, Rhythm,* or *Harmony* after number 1. Mark your answers quickly so that you will be ready to listen to the next song.

Playing the Games

One or more players can participate in the Youth Game or Adult Game. A CD player with good sound quality is needed to play the CD that accompanies the games. Answer sheets are included at the back of this book. Feel free to reproduce additional copies of the answer sheet as needed. When an adult is playing the game alone, he or she operates the CD player. If more than one adult is playing, one of the players should be designated to operate the CD player. When one or more children are playing the Youth Game, it is recommended that an adult operate the CD player.

Insert the CD into the CD player. If the Youth Game is being played, select Track 1. If the Adult Game is being played, select Track 2.

It is important that the game be played in a comfortable, quiet room. If a portable CD player is being used, but sure to place it in a spot where the CD can be heard clearly. The player or players will need a dark pencil with an eraser, a flat surface to write on, and the appropriate answer sheet provided with the games. Be sure to use the adult answer sheet with the Adult Game, and the youth answer sheet with the Youth Game.

Adults may want to read the game directions to young children before the recorded directions are played. Adults may also need to mark the answer sheet for young children when they are playing the game. If this is the case, then after the question, the children can tell the adult their answers. The adult should mark the answer sheet without having any discussion with the children.

Scoring the Games

The correct answers for both the Adult and Youth Games are found on page 31.

To score each game, count the number of correctly filled circles on the answer sheet, skipping all of the blank circles. The number that you come up with is the player's score. You may write the score on the answer sheet for future reference. Before scoring a young child's answer sheet, check to make sure that only one answer was marked for each question. If more than one circle is filled in for a question, the answer for that question should be struck out and not included in the final score. If a player has played the game without understanding the directions, the game may be played again once the directions are fully understood, without taking the previous score into consideration.

Interpreting the Scores

The objective results on the Youth and Adult Games represent general estimates of the extent of musical potential that you and your children possess. When interpreting the results, take into consideration that it is easier to obtain a high score on the Youth Game than on the Adult Game. For more specific information, one or more of the music aptitude tests listed in the next section can be used.

The scores, based on statistical analyses of the results of thousands of participants of varied ages and backgrounds in the United States who have played the Games, may be interpreted in the following manner:

	Youth Game	Adult Game
Excellent	38 to 40	36 to 40
Very Good	34 to 37	31 to 35
Average	27 to 33	20 to 30
Below Average	24 to 26	15 to 19
Fair	20 to 23	10 to 14

Because all of us have has at least some musical potential, everyone should be given the opportunity to learn and make music. Those who rank *Excellent* or *Very Good* may even want to consider pursuing music seriously. Singing, instrumental music, or movement instruction can prove to be both satisfying and rewarding. The key factor though is acquiring a knowledgeable teacher who is musical, and one who embraces the general ideas behind the psychology of music as well as the specific research in music learning theory. An informed teacher understands that both improvisation and the reading of music notation are important. Furthermore, the teacher realizes that it is best for students to engage in improvisation activities before learning to read music notation, and that instrumental and vocal technique should not be emphasized at the expense of the students' audiation development.

The results on the Youth Game should prove helpful to teachers and interested parents. Other than those who score high on the game, most players' results show diverse musical strengths and weaknesses. A student may be stronger in melody than in rhythm and/or harmony, stronger in rhythm than in melody and/or harmony, etc. In order to figure out a player's musical needs, scan the complete answer sheet, count how many blanks are filled in each column, then refer to the chart and the three sets of questions outlined below.

Melody	Rhythm	Harmony
1	4	3
8	5	7
9	11	12
16	13	19
20	14	21
24	23	22
29	26	27
31	32	33
36	34	35
39	40	38

- If 8 or more of the 10 circles are filled for the questions in the Melody column, that indicates strength in melodic audiation potential. If 8 or more of the 10 circles are blank for the questions in the Melody column, that indicates weakness in melodic audiation and potential.

- If 8 or more of the 10 circles are filled for the questions in the Rhythm column, that indicates strength in rhythm audiation and potential. If 8 or more of the 10 circles are blank for the questions in the Rhythm column, that indicates weakness in rhythm audiation and potential.

- If 8 or more of the 10 circles are filled for the questions in the Harmony column, that indicates strength in harmonic audiation and potential. If 8 or more of the 10 circles are blank for the questions in the Harmony column, that indicates weakness in harmonic audiation and potential.

Supplementary Music Aptitude Tests

If you choose to administer a supplementary standardized test of music aptitude, there are several choices, and they are all published by GIA Publications, Inc. Students in junior high and high school can use either the *Musical Aptitude Profile* or the *Advanced Measures of Music Audiation*, depending upon whether the extensive diagnostic information provided by the *Musical Aptitude Profile* is of importance at the time. Students in grades four to six can use either the *Music Aptitude Profile* or the *Intermediate Measures of Music Audiation,* although the *Music Aptitude Profile* offers greater reliability, and therefore greater precision, than the *Intermediate Measures of Music Audiation*. Also, the *Musical Aptitude Profile* is designed to provide greater diagnostic information than the two subtests for the *Intermediate Measures of Music Audiation*. Either the *Primary Measures of Music Audiation* or the *Intermediate Measures* of *Music Audiation* are suitable for students in grades one through three. The scores from the *Primary Measures of Music Audiation* can determine which test would be more suitable. If a child's score on the Primary Measures of Music Audiation is extremely high, then that child should take the *Intermediate Measures* of *Music Audiation* test just to cross check the scores. Finally, *Audie* may be used with children 3 or 4 years old.

To become thoroughly informed about the nature, description, measurement, and evaluation of music aptitudes, refer to the book titled *Introduction to Research and the Psychology of Music,* published by GIA Publications, Inc.

Question	Difficulty	Discrimination
1	89	38
2	90	32
3	50	33
4	90	34
5	91	35
6	92	51
7	55	44
8	94	40
9	90	57
10	93	52
11	89	50
12	90	59
13	72	47
14	92	52
15	93	36
16	90	49
17	96	50
18	93	40
19	78	51
20	92	49
21	55	50
22	49	44
23	93	47
24	80	50
25	95	38
26	86	40
27	76	63
28	95	46
29	80	38
30	92	36
31	82	42
32	89	36
33	60	50
34	92	40
35	65	48
36	80	32
37	95	30
38	73	43
39	90	53
40	92	56

Mean = 33.07   Standard Deviation = 4.02   Reliability = .91   Standard Error = 1.2
The correlation between the ages of students 7 through 12 with scores on the MAGS (*Music Audiation Games*) Youth Game is .16.

Question	Difficulty	Discrimination
1	83	54
2	91	54
3	61	44
4	92	59
5	82	55
6	92	61
7	86	64
8	82	60
9	75	52
10	93	54
11	89	62
12	85	54
13	84	45
14	81	49
15	95	55
16	82	47
17	95	56
18	93	44
19	81	64
20	82	56
21	85	59
22	73	60
23	83	46
24	82	53
25	93	51
26	66	40
27	82	44
28	95	43
29	76	44
30	95	30
31	76	38
32	79	36
33	83	51
34	60	30
35	74	50
36	60	35
37	95	30
38	73	40
39	80	51
40	88	44

Technical Information Adult Game

Mean = 33.5 Standard Deviation = 4.03 Reliability = .92 Standard Error = 1.2
The correlation between the ages of students 13 through adulthood with scores on the MAGS (*Music Audiation Games*) Adult Game is -.08.

Answer Key for the Youth Game

1. Not Same	11. Not Same	21. Not Same	31. Not Same
2. Same	12. Not Same	22. Not Same	32. Not Same
3. Not Same	13. Not Same	23. Not Same	33. Not Same
4. Not Same	14. Not Same	24. Not Same	34. Not Same
5. Not Same	15. Same	25. Same	35. Not Same
6. Same	16. Not Same	26. Not Same	36. Not Same
7. Not Same	17. Same	27. Not Same	37. Same
8. Not Same	18. Same	28. Same	38. Not Same
9. Not Same	19. Not Same	29. Not Same	39. Not Same
10. Same	20. Not Same	30. Same	40. Not Same

Answer Key the Adult Game

1. Melody	11. Rhythm	21. Harmony	31. Melody
2. Same	12. Harmony	22. Harmony	32. Rhythm
3. Harmony	13. Rhythm	23. Rhythm	33. Harmony
4. Rhythm	14. Rhythm	24. Melody	34. Rhythm
5. Rhythm	15. Same	25. Same	35. Harmony
6. Same	16. Melody	26. Rhythm	36. Melody
7. Harmony	17. Same	27. Harmony	37. Same
8. Melody	18. Same	28. Same	38. Harmony
9. Melody	19. Harmony	29. Melody	39. Melody
10. Same	20. Melody	30. Same	40. Rhythm

Youth Game *Answer Sheet*

Practice

Model			Model		
1.	Same ○	Not Same ○	3.	Same ○	Not Same ○
2.	Same ○	Not Same ○	4.	Same ○	Not Same ○

Begin

Model			Model		
1.	Same ○	Not Same ○	21.	Same ○	Not Same ○
2.	Same ○	Not Same ○	22.	Same ○	Not Same ○
Model			Model		
3.	Same ○	Not Same ○	23.	Same ○	Not Same ○
4.	Same ○	Not Same ○	24.	Same ○	Not Same ○
Model			Model		
5.	Same ○	Not Same ○	25.	Same ○	Not Same ○
6.	Same ○	Not Same ○	26.	Same ○	Not Same ○
Model			Model		
7.	Same ○	Not Same ○	27.	Same ○	Not Same ○
8.	Same ○	Not Same ○	28.	Same ○	Not Same ○
Model			Model		
9.	Same ○	Not Same ○	29.	Same ○	Not Same ○
10.	Same ○	Not Same ○	30.	Same ○	Not Same ○
Model			Model		
11.	Same ○	Not Same ○	31.	Same ○	Not Same ○
12.	Same ○	Not Same ○	32.	Same ○	Not Same ○
Model			Model		
13.	Same ○	Not Same ○	33.	Same ○	Not Same ○
14.	Same ○	Not Same ○	34.	Same ○	Not Same ○
Model			Model		
15.	Same ○	Not Same ○	35.	Same ○	Not Same ○
16.	Same ○	Not Same ○	36.	Same ○	Not Same ○
Model			Model		
17.	Same ○	Not Same ○	37.	Same ○	Not Same ○
18.	Same ○	Not Same ○	38.	Same ○	Not Same ○
Model			Model		
19.	Same ○	Not Same ○	39.	Same ○	Not Same ○
20.	Same ○	Not Same ○	40.	Same ○	Not Same ○

Music Audiation Games

Youth Game *Answer Sheet*

Practice

Model			Model		
1.	Same ○	Not Same ○	3.	Same ○	Not Same ○
2.	Same ○	Not Same ○	4.	Same ○	Not Same ○

Begin

Music Audiation Games

Model			Model		
1.	Same ○	Not Same ○	21.	Same ○	Not Same ○
2.	Same ○	Not Same ○	22.	Same ○	Not Same ○
Model			Model		
3.	Same ○	Not Same ○	23.	Same ○	Not Same ○
4.	Same ○	Not Same ○	24.	Same ○	Not Same ○
Model			Model		
5.	Same ○	Not Same ○	25.	Same ○	Not Same ○
6.	Same ○	Not Same ○	26.	Same ○	Not Same ○
Model			Model		
7.	Same ○	Not Same ○	27.	Same ○	Not Same ○
8.	Same ○	Not Same ○	28.	Same ○	Not Same ○
Model			Model		
9.	Same ○	Not Same ○	29.	Same ○	Not Same ○
10.	Same ○	Not Same ○	30.	Same ○	Not Same ○
Model			Model		
11.	Same ○	Not Same ○	31.	Same ○	Not Same ○
12.	Same ○	Not Same ○	32.	Same ○	Not Same ○
Model			Model		
13.	Same ○	Not Same ○	33.	Same ○	Not Same ○
14.	Same ○	Not Same ○	34.	Same ○	Not Same ○
Model			Model		
15.	Same ○	Not Same ○	35.	Same ○	Not Same ○
16.	Same ○	Not Same ○	36.	Same ○	Not Same ○
Model			Model		
17.	Same ○	Not Same ○	37.	Same ○	Not Same ○
18.	Same ○	Not Same ○	38.	Same ○	Not Same ○
Model			Model		
19.	Same ○	Not Same ○	39.	Same ○	Not Same ○
20.	Same ○	Not Same ○	40.	Same ○	Not Same ○

Youth Game *Answer Sheet*

Practice

Model			Model		
1.	Same ○	Not Same ○	3.	Same ○	Not Same ○
2.	Same ○	Not Same ○	4.	Same ○	Not Same ○

Begin

Model			Model		
1.	Same ○	Not Same ○	21.	Same ○	Not Same ○
2.	Same ○	Not Same ○	22.	Same ○	Not Same ○
Model			Model		
3.	Same ○	Not Same ○	23.	Same ○	Not Same ○
4.	Same ○	Not Same ○	24.	Same ○	Not Same ○
Model			Model		
5.	Same ○	Not Same ○	25.	Same ○	Not Same ○
6.	Same ○	Not Same ○	26.	Same ○	Not Same ○
Model			Model		
7.	Same ○	Not Same ○	27.	Same ○	Not Same ○
8.	Same ○	Not Same ○	28.	Same ○	Not Same ○
Model			Model		
9.	Same ○	Not Same ○	29.	Same ○	Not Same ○
10.	Same ○	Not Same ○	30.	Same ○	Not Same ○
Model			Model		
11.	Same ○	Not Same ○	31.	Same ○	Not Same ○
12.	Same ○	Not Same ○	32.	Same ○	Not Same ○
Model			Model		
13.	Same ○	Not Same ○	33.	Same ○	Not Same ○
14.	Same ○	Not Same ○	34.	Same ○	Not Same ○
Model			Model		
15.	Same ○	Not Same ○	35.	Same ○	Not Same ○
16.	Same ○	Not Same ○	36.	Same ○	Not Same ○
Model			Model		
17.	Same ○	Not Same ○	37.	Same ○	Not Same ○
18.	Same ○	Not Same ○	38.	Same ○	Not Same ○
Model			Model		
19.	Same ○	Not Same ○	39.	Same ○	Not Same ○
20.	Same ○	Not Same ○	40.	Same ○	Not Same ○

Music Audiation Games

Youth Game *Answer Sheet*

Practice

Model			Model	
1.	Same ⃝	Not Same ⃝	3.	Same ⃝	Not Same ⃝
2.	Same ⃝	Not Same ⃝	4.	Same ⃝	Not Same ⃝

Begin

Model			Model		
1.	Same ⃝	Not Same ⃝	21.	Same ⃝	Not Same ⃝
2.	Same ⃝	Not Same ⃝	22.	Same ⃝	Not Same ⃝
Model			Model		
3.	Same ⃝	Not Same ⃝	23.	Same ⃝	Not Same ⃝
4.	Same ⃝	Not Same ⃝	24.	Same ⃝	Not Same ⃝
Model			Model		
5.	Same ⃝	Not Same ⃝	25.	Same ⃝	Not Same ⃝
6.	Same ⃝	Not Same ⃝	26.	Same ⃝	Not Same ⃝
Model			Model		
7.	Same ⃝	Not Same ⃝	27.	Same ⃝	Not Same ⃝
8.	Same ⃝	Not Same ⃝	28.	Same ⃝	Not Same ⃝
Model			Model		
9.	Same ⃝	Not Same ⃝	29.	Same ⃝	Not Same ⃝
10.	Same ⃝	Not Same ⃝	30.	Same ⃝	Not Same ⃝
Model			Model		
11.	Same ⃝	Not Same ⃝	31.	Same ⃝	Not Same ⃝
12.	Same ⃝	Not Same ⃝	32.	Same ⃝	Not Same ⃝
Model			Model		
13.	Same ⃝	Not Same ⃝	33.	Same ⃝	Not Same ⃝
14.	Same ⃝	Not Same ⃝	34.	Same ⃝	Not Same ⃝
Model			Model		
15.	Same ⃝	Not Same ⃝	35.	Same ⃝	Not Same ⃝
16.	Same ⃝	Not Same ⃝	36.	Same ⃝	Not Same ⃝
Model			Model		
17.	Same ⃝	Not Same ⃝	37.	Same ⃝	Not Same ⃝
18.	Same ⃝	Not Same ⃝	38.	Same ⃝	Not Same ⃝
Model			Model		
19.	Same ⃝	Not Same ⃝	39.	Same ⃝	Not Same ⃝
20.	Same ⃝	Not Same ⃝	40.	Same ⃝	Not Same ⃝

Music Audiation Games

Adult Game *Answer Sheet*

Practice

	Same	Melody	Rhythm	Harmony		Same	Melody	Rhythm	Harmony
Model 1.	○	○	○	○	Model 3.	○	○	○	○
2.	○	○	○	○	4.	○	○	○	○

Begin

	Same	Melody	Rhythm	Harmony		Same	Melody	Rhythm	Harmony
Model 1.	○	○	○	○	Model 21.	○	○	○	○
2.	○	○	○	○	22.	○	○	○	○
Model 3.	○	○	○	○	Model 23.	○	○	○	○
4.	○	○	○	○	24.	○	○	○	○
Model 5.	○	○	○	○	Model 25.	○	○	○	○
6.	○	○	○	○	26.	○	○	○	○
Model 7.	○	○	○	○	Model 27.	○	○	○	○
8.	○	○	○	○	28.	○	○	○	○
Model 9.	○	○	○	○	Model 29.	○	○	○	○
10.	○	○	○	○	30.	○	○	○	○
Model 11.	○	○	○	○	Model 31.	○	○	○	○
12.	○	○	○	○	32.	○	○	○	○
Model 13.	○	○	○	○	Model 33.	○	○	○	○
14.	○	○	○	○	34.	○	○	○	○
Model 15.	○	○	○	○	Model 35.	○	○	○	○
16.	○	○	○	○	36.	○	○	○	○
Model 17.	○	○	○	○	Model 37.	○	○	○	○
18.	○	○	○	○	38.	○	○	○	○
Model 19.	○	○	○	○	Model 39.	○	○	○	○
20.	○	○	○	○	40.	○	○	○	○

Music Audiation Games

Adult Game *Answer Sheet*

Practice

	Same	Melody	Rhythm	Harmony		Same	Melody	Rhythm	Harmony
Model 1. 2.	○ ○	○ ○	○ ○	○ ○	Model 3. 4.	○ ○	○ ○	○ ○	○ ○

Begin

	Same	Melody	Rhythm	Harmony		Same	Melody	Rhythm	Harmony
Model 1. 2.	○ ○	○ ○	○ ○	○ ○	Model 21. 22.	○ ○	○ ○	○ ○	○ ○
Model 3. 4.	○ ○	○ ○	○ ○	○ ○	Model 23. 24.	○ ○	○ ○	○ ○	○ ○
Model 5. 6.	○ ○	○ ○	○ ○	○ ○	Model 25. 26.	○ ○	○ ○	○ ○	○ ○
Model 7. 8.	○ ○	○ ○	○ ○	○ ○	Model 27. 28.	○ ○	○ ○	○ ○	○ ○
Model 9. 10.	○ ○	○ ○	○ ○	○ ○	Model 29. 30.	○ ○	○ ○	○ ○	○ ○
Model 11. 12.	○ ○	○ ○	○ ○	○ ○	Model 31. 32.	○ ○	○ ○	○ ○	○ ○
Model 13. 14.	○ ○	○ ○	○ ○	○ ○	Model 33. 34.	○ ○	○ ○	○ ○	○ ○
Model 15. 16.	○ ○	○ ○	○ ○	○ ○	Model 35. 36.	○ ○	○ ○	○ ○	○ ○
Model 17. 18.	○ ○	○ ○	○ ○	○ ○	Model 37. 38.	○ ○	○ ○	○ ○	○ ○
Model 19. 20.	○ ○	○ ○	○ ○	○ ○	Model 39. 40.	○ ○	○ ○	○ ○	○ ○

Music Audiation Games

Adult Game *Answer Sheet*

Practice

	Same	Melody	Rhythm	Harmony		Same	Melody	Rhythm	Harmony
Model 1. 2.	○○	○○	○○	○○	Model 3. 4.	○○	○○	○○	○○

Begin

	Same	Melody	Rhythm	Harmony		Same	Melody	Rhythm	Harmony
Model 1. 2.	○○	○○	○○	○○	Model 21. 22.	○○	○○	○○	○○
Model 3. 4.	○○	○○	○○	○○	Model 23. 24.	○○	○○	○○	○○
Model 5. 6.	○○	○○	○○	○○	Model 25. 26.	○○	○○	○○	○○
Model 7. 8.	○○	○○	○○	○○	Model 27. 28.	○○	○○	○○	○○
Model 9. 10.	○○	○○	○○	○○	Model 29. 30.	○○	○○	○○	○○
Model 11. 12.	○○	○○	○○	○○	Model 31. 32.	○○	○○	○○	○○
Model 13. 14.	○○	○○	○○	○○	Model 33. 34.	○○	○○	○○	○○
Model 15. 16.	○○	○○	○○	○○	Model 35. 36.	○○	○○	○○	○○
Model 17. 18.	○○	○○	○○	○○	Model 37. 38.	○○	○○	○○	○○
Model 19. 20.	○○	○○	○○	○○	Model 39. 40.	○○	○○	○○	○○

Music Audiation Games

Adult Game *Answer Sheet*

Practice

	Same	Melody	Rhythm	Harmony		Same	Melody	Rhythm	Harmony
Model 1. 2.	○ ○	○ ○	○ ○	○ ○	Model 3. 4.	○ ○	○ ○	○ ○	○ ○

Begin

	Same	Melody	Rhythm	Harmony		Same	Melody	Rhythm	Harmony
Model 1. 2.	○ ○	○ ○	○ ○	○ ○	Model 21. 22.	○ ○	○ ○	○ ○	○ ○
Model 3. 4.	○ ○	○ ○	○ ○	○ ○	Model 23. 24.	○ ○	○ ○	○ ○	○ ○
Model 5. 6.	○ ○	○ ○	○ ○	○ ○	Model 25. 26.	○ ○	○ ○	○ ○	○ ○
Model 7. 8.	○ ○	○ ○	○ ○	○ ○	Model 27. 28.	○ ○	○ ○	○ ○	○ ○
Model 9. 10.	○ ○	○ ○	○ ○	○ ○	Model 29. 30.	○ ○	○ ○	○ ○	○ ○
Model 11. 12.	○ ○	○ ○	○ ○	○ ○	Model 31. 32.	○ ○	○ ○	○ ○	○ ○
Model 13. 14.	○ ○	○ ○	○ ○	○ ○	Model 33. 34.	○ ○	○ ○	○ ○	○ ○
Model 15. 16.	○ ○	○ ○	○ ○	○ ○	Model 35. 36.	○ ○	○ ○	○ ○	○ ○
Model 17. 18.	○ ○	○ ○	○ ○	○ ○	Model 37. 38.	○ ○	○ ○	○ ○	○ ○
Model 19. 20.	○ ○	○ ○	○ ○	○ ○	Model 39. 40.	○ ○	○ ○	○ ○	○ ○

Music Audiation Games

About the Author

Edwin E. Gordon is known as perhaps the world's preeminent researcher, teacher, author, editor, and lecturer in the field of music education.

Through extensive research, Professor Gordon has made major contributions to the study of music aptitudes, stages and types of audiation, music learning theory, and rhythm in movement and music, to name just a few endeavors.

Following his retirement as the Carl E. Seashore Professor of Research in Music Education at Temple University in Philadelphia in 1997, Dr. Gordon has served at both the Univerity of South Carolina and Michigan State University.

In addition to advising Ph.D. candidates in music education, Dr. Gordon has devoted many years to teaching music to pre-school aged children.

Before devoting his life to the field of music education, he earned bachelor's and master's degrees in string bass performance from the Eastman School of Music and played string bass with the Gene Krupa band. He went on to earn a Ph.D. from the University of Iowa in 1958.

Professor Gordon and his work have been portrayed nationally and internationally on the NBC Today Show, in the New York Times, in USA Today, and in a variety of European and Asian publications.

He lives with his wife Carol in Columbia, South Carolina.